RECRUITING & SELECTION

Albert Houpy & T.J. Schier

This book is dedicated to my wife Lisa.
Her understanding and unwavering love and support
over the past 25 years has afforded me the opportunity
to commit the time and effort necessary to build
a successful career within the restaurant industry.

Published by

For more information on S.M.A.R.T. Restaurant Guidebooks, call 972-691-7378
www.smartrestaurantguides.com

CONTENTS

PREFACE

By now, hopefully you have read the *S.M.A.R.T. Restaurant Guide to Effective Food Service Operations*—the "foundation" book in the S.M.A.R.T. Restaurant Guidebook series. Subsequent "pillar" books such as this one are designed to provide more of a "deep dive" into some of the critical business drivers for restaurant success. One of those key pillars to building a successful restaurant or restaurant company is recruiting and selecting S.M.A.R.T.-*er* employees and managers.

Albert Houpy, the primary author of this book, has spent more than three decades as an operator, multi-unit supervisor, professional recruiter and director of operations. Heck, he was my boss for a long time and things have now come full circle as we work together on building the S.M.A.R.T. Restaurant Group.

Having worked on both the operations and recruiting side of the restaurant business, Albert's insights provide simple, effective strategies to help you build a S.M.A.R.T.-*er* team.

Building off the 25 keys presented in the *S.M.A.R.T. Restaurant Guide to Effective Food Service Operations,* this book expands on the following keys:

S	**M**
1-Sales	**6-Mission**
2-Service	7-Management
3-Selection	8-Measurement/Metrics
4-Systems	9-Marketing
5-Speed	10-Mastery

A
11-Accuracy
12-Accountability
13-Accept/Adapt/Apply
14-Assessment
15-Attraction

R
16-Roadmap
17-Reinforcement
18-Recognition
19-Rewarding
20-Results

T
21-Talent
22-Training
23-Technology
24-Tools
25-Trust

These 25 keys set the foundation for success. It is now time to start recruiting and selecting a S.M.A.R.T.-*er* team. What does that talent look like? Where do you find them? Will they fit in? What sort of systems should you follow? All valid questions...and ones that are answered in the following pages.

Read on, be S.M.A.R.T.-*er* and prosper!

—T.J. Schier

INTRODUCTION
THE MOTHER OF ALL DECISIONS

It's Monday morning, and as I pull into the restaurant parking lot for my morning shift, I do a quick mental review of everything I need to accomplish for the day. Being the General Manager I enjoy the responsibility of running my business, but can't help feeling overwhelmed at times with all that is expected of me. But I have a plan, and this is the beginning of a new week.

As I enter the building and do my initial walk-through my optimism begins to fade. My kitchen closer last night missed quite a few items. Unfortunately, my on-again–off-again Assistant Manager appears to have had an off night last night. I hired my new cook only 5 days ago after the abrupt departure of his predecessor for personal reasons. No worries though—I can handle this situation. Just a few adjustments to the morning routine and we will be ready to open on time.

Wait a minute, where is my opening cook? She is late again! Her tardiness frustrates me to no end. She is a great prep cook and works hard, but just cannot seem to get to work on time. No need to panic—I tell myself—give her a wake-up call, get the prep station set up and get to work. As I work feverishly on the fresh prep for the day I can't help but wish there was another opening cook to call in to work. The opener eventually makes it to work, and we hustle to get the day's prep complete just in time to swing our doors open.

As I start organizing my team for the day, I remember we have to run lunch one person short, which forces me to adjust the sections for the team. It is a risky move, knowing it could overload my less-experienced servers, but there is nobody else to bring in to cover the shift. I quickly huddle up my team and set expectations for the day. By now I'm feeling pretty good about myself—overcoming some hurdles and ready for a successful shift. Bring it on!

Knowing the server shortage, I am hands-on: expediting orders, filling drinks and settling checks. Things seem to be humming right along when a server says, "My table wants to speak with the manager." I quickly walk over to the guest's table to be told that we have made a mistake on their appetizer. The guest just couldn't understand how we could serve crab-stuffed mushrooms, without any crab. In her haste to get things done this morning, the opening cook apparently forgot to add the crabmeat to the stuffing mix.

A little magic wins over this guest, and we let the hosts and servers know to inform guests that the crab-stuffed mushrooms are not available for lunch today. OK, problem solved. A few other minor guest challenges resolved throughout lunch and we survive the rush. As lunch winds down, things are finally back under control.

By the time I completed my shift administration and communicated with my on-again–off-again Assistant Manager about the expectations for tonight's shift, my day was done. Leaving the parking lot, I do a mental recap of my day. I feel satisfied I managed all of the shift's adversity effectively, but am nagged by the fact that our service quality was less than WOW!, and the staff was quite stressed dealing with the shortage and mistakes.

I have a very clear vision of the guest experience and an equally clear vision of what I want my employees to experience: the challenge is finding dependable cooks who are on time and detail-oriented, a competent wait staff that is hospitality-driven and Assistant Managers who can drive standards. Is that asking too much? After all, those three things could achieve the vision for my guests as well as my employees.

The Background

The preceding anecdote is a story I have seen played out many times over a 30-year restaurant industry career. As a long-time multi-unit operator, recruiting professional and General Manager, I have experienced it first-hand as a GM, through GMs running restaurants under my leadership

INTRODUCTION

and through CEOs and presidents of companies I have consulted with. These stories can have a happy ending. Regardless of your scope of responsibility, as a restaurant leader you have the ability to write that happy ending. Although hundreds of books on the subject of effective management and leadership have been written describing the "steps" to effective management or leadership, there is a common denominator across all these books—the importance of people. Nobody can effectively run a restaurant alone!

Over many years working with presidents and CEOs in fine dining, casual dining, fast casual, family dining, and QSR, there is one question I always ask leadership, "What is the biggest problem you face in achieving your financial goals?" The answer is universal: "People". The consensus? Having the "right" people would make a difference to the bottom line of at least 10% to 20%! As restaurant leaders we are decision makers. Some decisions are big, others small. Some are spur-of-the-moment, others more deliberate. The ability to adequately deliberate on the *right* decisions allows one to write the happy ending to our story. And the mother of all decisions is who we hire.

Restaurant operators know the negative effects an understaffed restaurant has on sales, service, profits and people. S.M.A.R.T. managers are also aware of the negative effects a fully staffed restaurant with the *wrong* people has as well. The wrong people cannot maximize sales and profit potential. S.M.A.R.T. managers will not accept an unhappy ending or too many shifts from hell.

This book outlines the recruitment and selection process to help you as a S.M.A.R.T. manager make an effective and successful hiring decision. Whether you are responsible for staffing hourly team members, unit management, multi-unit or executive-level, the principles are the same—a detailed, thoughtful process that leads to a successful hiring decision.

CHAPTER 1
DON'T PLAY DARTS IN THE DARK

If selecting and hiring people were an exact science, life would be much easier for everyone—more free time to sit on a beach somewhere and enjoy some of those extra earnings not currently being produced. If selection were as simple as a formula, restaurant leaders would have solved the perennial "people" challenge. But it is not an exact science, and finding that perfect fit with every person hired will not always happen.

S.M.A.R.T. managers, however, are disciplined in the search and commit the time to this important decision necessary to significantly improve results. The selection process is much like throwing darts. Too often, managers hire blindly—similar to playing darts in the dark. It's hard to hit the bull's-eye when one cannot see the target! Revolving door of employees parading in and out of the restaurant? Why are people leaving? Wrong talent fit? Not the right person? Lack of specific skills needed for success? Maybe the person just didn't "fit in". Maybe the person found an opportunity that better fit their needs. Regardless of the reason we just continue to miss the mark on our hiring decisions. Stop playing darts in the dark!

Why does a S.M.A.R.T. manager have a much higher level of success? They can see the dartboard. They have practiced hitting the bull's-eye and know what they are looking for. The S.M.A.R.T. manager generally hires people who not only possess the necessary skills and talents for the position, but also who have the values and career/personal goals required to be a successful, long-term fit. Though the S.M.A.R.T. manager will also miss the bull's-eye on occasion, it is frequently by a lesser degree.

Though both managers are playing the same game of darts, the first is playing in the dark while the S.M.A.R.T. manager chooses to turn the lights on. The first operator is frustrated how infrequently he hits the bull's-eye, let alone the board at all! Since the S.M.A.R.T. manager can see where they are aiming, at least they hit the board with far more regularity.

Said another way, the S.M.A.R.T. manager will need far fewer throws of the dart to fill their needs. Throwing less darts to achieve success frees up the manager's time to work on other critical elements such as training and marketing. Meanwhile, the first operator is still blindly throwing darts and continuing the turnover carousel.

The darts in this analogy represent each hiring decision. S.M.A.R.T. managers know there are four lights needed to "illuminate the dartboard" (and improve hiring success):

- Experience required
- Qualities and traits required
- Core values
- Personal/career fit

When the S.M.A.R.T. manager throws the dart with the benefit of these lights, it is thrown with confidence. Not there yet? Understanding the "four lights" is the first step to improving the success ratio.

The process to recruit and hire people starts with clearly defining exactly who to hire. S.M.A.R.T. managers develop a profile for each specific position in the restaurant.

- What are the minimum skills and experience required to be successful in the position? From that group of people who possess those skills...
- What are the personal qualities and traits that are necessary for success? From this even smaller group...
- Identify the values making a new hire an organizational fit. To help ensure the longevity of our new hire's tenure,
- Ensure their personal or career goals are congruent with what the position offers.

Let's start turning on the lights...

Experience

Though templates for skills needed by position are available, no two concepts are the same. For example:

- The skills needed for a server at a family dining restaurant specializing in breakfast might not necessarily translate to success at a high-end steak house with an extensive wine menu.
- An experienced cashier from a fast casual concept may not have the skills necessary to be a successful cashier at a QSR with a drive-thru window.
- A GM with experience operating a quick service restaurant might lack some of necessary skills to have success operating a casual dining restaurant.

In determining exactly who to hire, the S.M.A.R.T. manager assesses what experience is necessary to achieve a high level of success at each position in the restaurant. Though previous work experience is certainly desired, it may not be necessary depending on the position…and a candidate with previous experience may lack some skills necessary to have success in your restaurant.

S.M.A.R.T. managers develop a specific hiring profile for each position in the restaurant. The first step in developing a profile is identifying the importance of experience. For example, experience may not be necessary for a dishwasher or host (but is definitely needed in other positions). Experience (for example, 1–2 years) may be absolutely necessary for line-cook positions. Servers may need at least 2 years' experience specific to casual dining.

The S.M.A.R.T. manager will begin the hiring profiles with clear determination of any minimum experience levels required for the position. Here are a few examples of experience levels required for the following positions within a restaurant (see next page):

HOST	COOK
No experience required	Minimum of 2 years line-cook experience
KM	**AM**
Minimum 2 years KM experience	Minimum 2 years FOH mgmt. experience

To many managers, determining the necessary experience level for each position completes their hiring profile. They are ready to interview. For S.M.A.R.T. managers, experience is only the beginning.

Qualities and Traits

In a past life as a recruiting specialist, I saw many hiring profiles for similar positions. Some companies had no profiles at all! There was a direct correlation between the various hiring profiles and the reasons companies were seeking my help:

- Companies seeking help to grow generally had a very detailed hiring profile.
- Companies seeking help with difficulty keeping up with turnover generally had very simple hiring profiles. For example:
    - At least 2 years of experience in the position
    - No more than 3 jobs over the past 5 years
    - Within a specified salary range

If the restaurant has no hiring profile or a simple one, such as this one, spend time developing a more detailed hiring profile immediately. S.M.A.R.T. managers build a profile of their top performers—what differentiates the top 10% of performers from the pack? Build a profile based on the common-thread qualities and traits of these top performers. This process is crucial if you want to do more than just fill a hole.

The S.M.A.R.T. manager's goal in hiring is to come as close as possible to "cloning" their top performers. This hiring profile is the "DNA" needed to start the cloning process. So how do you start creating the profile?

DON'T PLAY DARTS IN THE DARK

Do you operate a single restaurant or are you responsible for the service or kitchen management? Seek input from the entire management team in the restaurant. Multi-unit supervisor? Get input from all the GMs. The key is to collectively build this profile. As a team, ask two simple questions:

1. Who are the top 10% of performers in each specific position?
2. What traits make them exceptional at what they do?

Review person-by-person in each position, and list their many qualities and traits. Common threads will become evident. The profile of the qualities and traits desired for each position can be quickly built. Here is an example of what such a profile might look like for various positions:

HOST	COOK	KITCHEN MANAGER	ASSISTANT MANAGER
Great image	Drive/energy	Drive/energy	Drive/energy
Communication skills	Urgency	Urgency	Urgency
Outgoing/ friendly	Attention to detail	Attention to detail	Attention to detail
Organizational skills	Ability to multi-task	Ability to multi-task	Ability to multi-task
	Follows recipes	Communication skills/bilingual?	Communication skills
		Good with numbers	Service/ hospitality-oriented
		Accountable	Image/ appearance
			Problem solving

As the S.M.A.R.T. manager develops position-specific hiring profiles, a giant step has been taken to begin the cloning process of the top performers. Most of what we have defined about our desired candidates to this point is what they *do*. But the S.M.A.R.T. manager also recognizes the importance of *how* a person does what he or she does. What are this person's core values, and how closely do they resemble mine?

5

Core Values

Gary Zancanelli best illustrates the importance of core values. Gary was president of ZMC, which operated YUM! Brand restaurants. In 2006, his company consisted of 35 restaurants—growing from 5 locations only 6 years earlier. His plans were to continue his growth at a more accelerated level. While other companies imploded trying to grow quickly (without the proper human capital), Gary was S.M.A.R.T.

Gary was not growing just for growth's sake; he wanted to build an exceptional company. Gary has a deep appreciation for his people. He knew the only way he could achieve his aggressive growth goals was through high performing people. Nothing will slow down growth plans faster than hiring mistakes. Gary needed exceptional people at all levels, from his executive team, to multi-unit operators, to unit level managers, to front-line crew members.

As mentioned previously, incomplete (or lack of) hiring profiles causes too many hiring mistakes. The person hired may possess all of the experience, qualities and traits to make them successful. But when they start working, they somehow just don't "fit in". The problem is not the lack of the raw skill, talent and experience to be successful in the restaurant. Many times the problem is they lack the values to be successful within your team. S.M.A.R.T. managers understand the importance of clear values and hiring those people who will "fit in".

Gary not only developed very specific profiles for each position; he also shared the company's mission statement. The clarity of his company mission and core values made it much easier to find people who had not only the necessary skills and experience, but who also shared the values of Gary and his team.

ZMC VISION, MISSION AND CORE VALUES

Every Customer Leaves Happy...
Our mission is to maintain a passion for excellence. We are committed to creating the ultimate in customer satisfaction by developing our people through superior implementation of training and systems. We are a socially responsible, integrity driven company and we strive to be better each and every day.

We praise efforts, recognize progress, and reward results.
- We value the commitment, intensity, focus, and drive it takes to be successful.

- We care enough about each other to give honest feedback about behavior and results.

- We are a results-orientated company.

All decisions must benefit the company, team, and ultimately the individual.
- Use data to help guide your decisions.

- We are committed to creating win-win situations for all.

- Winning together is better than winning alone.

- Utilize the team around you to help make decisions.

The worst decision is to make no decision.
- Decisions that ensure our customers leave happy are good decisions.

- Decisions that ensure our employees are happy are good decisions.

- It is OK to make mistakes. Own and learn from them.

Our success is measured by the development and success of those we serve.
- Loyalty flows downward.

- Respect for each other is essential.

- We want each person to achieve their highest potential.

Gary had very clearly articulated his mission and the values by which he and his team went about their daily activities (how they think; how they do what they do). This mission statement was much more than just a bunch of words on a piece of paper. He and his team walked their talk.

Though recruiting is never easy (we had to interview dozens and dozens of candidates for each position to send just a small handful of finalists to Gary and his team), Gary made it easy in the sense we *knew* when we found a great match for his company. We spoke with many managers and executives having the experience that Gary was looking for, but if they did not passionately share his values, they would not succeed.

Gary truly approached his hiring decisions as the mother of all decisions. And at the end of 2011 Gary had grown his company to 81 locations. S.M.A.R.T. managers do as Gary did. They very clearly define the values most describing their restaurant or their company. These values become part of the profile built for *all* positions. A S.M.A.R.T. manager will include these core values as part of the hiring profile. If the company does not yet have a mission statement, the S.M.A.R.T. manager will develop a mission specific to his restaurant or area of responsibility. Operating without a clear mission is like setting sail without a map or like a GPS in a boat with no rudder!

Incorporating the key values of ZMC into the hiring profile, one might end up with the following position-specific hiring profiles (see next page):

DON'T PLAY DARTS IN THE DARK

HOST	COOK
No experience required	*Minimum of 2 years line cook experience*
Service-oriented	Service-oriented
Desire to improve/advance	Desire to improve/advance
Results-oriented	Results-oriented
Decisive	Decisive
Great image	Drive/energy
Communication skills	Urgency
Outgoing/friendly	Attention to detail
Organizational skills	Ability to multi-task

KITCHEN MANAGER	ASSISTANT MANAGER
Minimum 2 years KM experience	*Minimum 2 years FOH mgmt. experience*
Passion for guest service	Passion for guest service
Passion for people development	Passion for people development
Appreciates effort/rewards results	Appreciates effort/rewards results
Decisive	Decisive
Drive/energy	Drive/energy
Urgency	Urgency
Attention to detail	Attention to detail
Ability to multi-task	Ability to multi-task
Communication skills	Communication skills
Good with numbers	Service/hospitality-oriented
Accountable	Image/appearance
	Problem solving

The experience required has been defined along with the qualities and traits desired. Coupled with the core values, the hiring profile is almost complete. The last important piece we need to make a hiring decision standing the greatest chance of netting a long-term employee lies with each individual candidate.

Personal/Career Fit

The final factor S.M.A.R.T. managers consider before making a hiring decision is personal/career fit. There are times when it may be a wise decision *not* to extend an offer to a candidate that has the exact experience looked for, combined with the qualities and traits and an alignment with your core values.

As operators, one understands and appreciates the importance of tenure. S.M.A.R.T. managers understand the effect turnover has on operations and the bottom line. The objective of the S.M.A.R.T. manager in making a hiring decision is not only to hire candidates who will be highly successful, but also to hire those who will be long-term.

The average operator may view it as "bad luck" when an employee is hired away by another company, had to quit for school, or moved to another town. Sometimes bad luck does strike. The S.M.A.R.T. manager chooses to do everything possible to take luck out of the equation. Trying to fill an important day-cook position? The S.M.A.R.T. manager may not extend an offer to an otherwise excellent applicant who plans on moving at the end of the year. Or, as perfect a fit that a manager applicant may seem, the S.M.A.R.T. manager may not extend an offer if he knows he cannot provide the career growth over the next two years that the applicant desires.

The S.M.A.R.T. manager is careful to match the needs of the restaurant (part time, full time, seasonal, permanent, fast track, entry level, salary range, etc.) with the applicants' desires. Where those needs and desires intersect is where the highest probability of success occurs (taking luck out of the equation). The S.M.A.R.T. manager develops hiring profiles to provide clarity toward the type of candidate who will have success within the restaurant. It is also important to clearly see all aspects of each specific position being hired for, from the perspective of the candidate. What does the applicant desire in a job? What does the applicant desire in an employer? What does the applicant desire in a career?

DON'T PLAY DARTS IN THE DARK

The S.M.A.R.T. manager clearly defines these specific aspects as the final touches to the hiring profile. This allows the manager to more clearly identify those candidates whose desires are most aligned with the needs of the restaurant. The final hiring profile may look as follows:

Hiring Profile For: HOST	
This opening is: __ seasonal _x_ permanent _x_ part time __ full time **Pay range:** $8.00–$8.50/hour	Service-oriented Desire to improve/advance Results-oriented Decisive Great Image Communication skills Outgoing/friendly Organizational skills
Hiring Profile For: ASSISTANT MANAGER	
This opening is: __ seasonal _x_ permanent __ part time _x_ full time **Pay range:** $38K–$40K (salary)	Passion for guest service Passion for people development Appreciates effort; rewards results Decisive Drive/energy Urgency Attention to detail Ability to multi-task Communication skills Service/hospitality-oriented Image/appearance Problem solving

With a detailed hiring profile, the restaurant operator has greatly increased his or her probability of success in making hiring decisions. But the S.M.A.R.T. manager also appreciates the importance of timing in making hiring decisions. The next chapter will address how the S.M.A.R.T. manager stays proactive in his or her recruiting efforts, and avoids the crisis hire. For sample position templates, visit www.smartrestaurantguides.com.

CHAPTER 2
BEGGARS CAN'T BE CHOOSERS

Successful restaurant managers appreciate the importance of maintaining accurate par levels to the success of their daily operations. Place a food order without accurate par levels or without taking a count? You're likely going to run out of some items while having too many of others. Do daily prep without par levels on hand? You're guaranteed to run out of some product in the middle of rush or have too much left over.

S.M.A.R.T. managers ensure balance between not running out of any product and having too much. Maintaining ideal staffing levels is no different. The manpower plan is a par level sheet for staffing. S.M.A.R.T. managers always maintain an updated manpower plan no matter if the scope of responsibility is one restaurant or an entire company.

Managers order on set schedules versus waiting to run out of a product prior to ordering. The approach to staffing should be no different. Take the time necessary to be selective and hire only those candidates who fit the hiring profile and one will avoid being put into a crisis situation. As one would not wait until we serve the last hamburger before ordering more, S.M.A.R.T. managers do not wait until there is a vacancy to fill a position. When under the gun to make a hiring decision, managers sacrifice certain aspects of the hiring profile to fill an urgent need. S.M.A.R.T. managers understand that beggars can't be choosers

Many restaurant operators believe the most cost-effective approach (short-term) to hiring is to wait until a position is open to fill it. By taking this approach they will reduce their labor cost, right? The S.M.A.R.T. manager will always choose long-term gain over short-term reward. Short staffed? S.M.A.R.T. managers make adjustments to deal with a vacant position. Otherwise guests, team members and investors will feel the impact in the following ways:

- Guests can experience the pain of the vacant position through operational missteps as a result of running short.
- Team members can experience the pain of the vacant position through the increased stress of a heavier workload and longer hours.
- Investors can experience the pain of the vacant position through a loss of sales and efficiencies as a result of these missteps and increased workloads.

What happens next can compound the pain felt by guests, team members and investors exponentially. When filling a vacant position with someone who does not meet the hiring profile, the proverbial "weak link" has just been brought into the company. The problems may not be as overt as they are when operating shorthanded, but they exist nonetheless.

Now the decision made by the manager has a slow corrosive effect on operations and financial performance—slowly eating away at the execution of product quality and guest service. All the while it creates small holes of inefficiencies in the costs of goods sold as well as productivity. Though every opening cannot be predicted before it happens, the S.M.A.R.T. manager avoids crisis-hiring situations through manpower planning.

An effective manpower plan will consist of four components:

1. Employee Ranking
2. Employee Assessment
3. Projected Turnover
4. Hiring Needs

Employee Ranking and Assessment

The first step in preparing a manpower plan is to rank each member of the team in each position. Start with the best performer at the top of the list, followed by each member of the team listed in order of performance—much like a band director might list the "chairs" for each instrument or like a basketball or football coach might create the "depth chart" by position.

The next step is to do a quick assessment of the members of each position. Assign a letter grade to each team member, having each member of management rank each person. The management team needs clarity on each employee and to discuss any differences. As an employee, it would be difficult to be an "A" in one manager's eyes and a "C" in another. Assess each person's performance measured against an "A", "B" or "C" level of performance:

> **A: This person is a consistent top performer. They meet all of the qualities and traits of the position and produce consistent, high-quality results. This player is one you would like to "clone".**

> **B: This person is a good performer. They may lack the consistency the A-players produce because they are less experienced or deficient in some of the qualities and traits needed for the position. This group shows the ability to improve upon these deficiencies when given direction.**

> **C: This person is an underperformer. Many times they are chronic underperformers. Usually there are obvious deficiencies in qualities and traits.**

This assessment will help the S.M.A.R.T. manager not only produce an effective manpower plan, but also aid in producing a developmental plan for the existing employees. As the S.M.A.R.T. manager goes through this simple process of ranking and assessing employees, it makes it easier to more accurately and proactively predict turnover and plan for "upgrades" within each position.

Projected Turnover

There are two steps to projecting turnover on the manpower plan—an objective step and a subjective step. The objective step involves a simple math equation. S.M.A.R.T. managers always measure turnover—ideally on a monthly basis. Just as a S.M.A.R.T. manager has a high level of awareness as to sales and profit trends, he or she is also highly aware of her turnover trends.

Turnover percentage should be measured monthly and annualized to gauge performance. Similar to sales and profits trends over time, patterns emerge for turnover as well. To be proactive at the unit level, project turnover for employees out three months.

At the management level and above, the time horizon can be anywhere from 3 to 12 months, depending on such factors as the number of restaurants and projected growth.

Calculating Turnover Examples

To illustrate how to calculate turnover, use the following assumptions:
- Current annualized turnover results of 80%
- Current staffing level of 50 employees

At a turnover rate of 80%, this restaurant will turn over 40 employees in a year—3.3 employees per month, or a projected 3-month turnover of 10 employees. S.M.A.R.T. managers base projected turnover on the current actual trends versus projected or desired trends (that strategy is simply "wishing"). This approach is a very objective prediction based on the current results.

The second step to turnover projection is somewhat subjective. Refer to the list of all 50 employees, ranked by position. Knowing that approximately 10 of those employees will be lost over the next 3 months, identify which 10 employees are most likely not going to be employed at the restaurant in 3 months.

See the next page for an example of what a manpower plan might look like for a specific position.

BEGGARS CAN'T BE CHOOSERS

RANK	PREP NAME	GRADE	PROJECTED T.O.
1	Bob	A	
2	Barbara	A	
3	Miguel	A	
4	Janet	B	
5	John	B	X
6	Ross	B	
7	Ryan	B	
8	Jack	B	
9	Jane	C	
10	Travis	C	X
		TOTALS	2

Our manpower plan is almost complete. Each current player is ranked by position and assessed by their current overall performance level. Turnover has been calculated for the next 3 months, and the managers have identified specific positions within the restaurant needing to be filled. We now have all of the information needed to accurately calculate our hiring needs and complete our manpower plan. The formula to calculate hiring needs is as follows:

Turnover Calculation Formula
(ideal staffing) + (projected turnover) – (current staff) = Needs

In our example restaurant, let's assume that our ideal staffing level is 52 and our current staffing level is 50. Based on our 3-month projected turnover the hiring plan is as follows:

$$
\begin{array}{ll}
\text{Staffing needs} & 52 \\
(+) & \\
\text{Projected T.O.} & 10 \\
(-) & \\
\text{Current level} & 50 \\
(=) & \\
\text{Hiring needs} & 12 \\
\end{array}
$$

Hiring Needs

S.M.A.R.T. managers know the turnover percentage will not be applied evenly across each position. Why? Because many times a vacancy can be filled through succession planning. For example, if you are projecting the loss of a prep cook within the next 3 months, should you hire a new prep cook? Perhaps not. Knowing the succession plan, maybe you have a busser who you believe possesses the qualities and traits to make a good prep cook. The S.M.A.R.T. manager might make the decision to hire a busboy instead of a prep cook. This step of the planning process also helps the S.M.A.R.T. manager gain a clearer sense for which positions might be open first or are of higher priority.

Additionally, the S.M.A.R.T. manager may choose to upgrade a C-player. Relying solely on the number of ten hires needed overall does not provide any sense of where to start.

This plan allows the S.M.A.R.T. manager to maintain a 3-month time horizon to recruit and select employees. In this case, the restaurant needs to hire on average one person per week to achieve the staffing goal. More specifically by reviewing the rankings and projected turnover by position the S.M.A.R.T. manager knows how to prioritize the weekly recruiting efforts.

Instead of just going after 12 hires, the S.M.A.R.T. manager can concentrate efforts on specific high priority needs first. This process helps avoid crisis-hiring situations, and allows the S.M.A.R.T. manager to take the time necessary to adequately assess whether or not applicants fit the specific hiring profiles.

After the S.M.A.R.T. manager has prioritized which positions to recruit for and has developed a very clear profile, the process can begin. We know who we want; now where do we find them?

CHAPTER 3

TROUT FISHING ON LAKE TEXOMA

One of my all-time favorite recreational activities is fishing. One of the earliest memories I have as a small child was catching trout. My family lived close to a stream that was a tributary for the Green River in Washington State. All you need to catch trout is fishing line, a hook and some night crawlers and you can be catching fish. Some days I caught buckets of trout using some fishing line with a hook tied to a stick. If only recruiting were so easy!

Fast-forward to today—living in north Texas just a 1-hour drive from Lake Texoma on the Texas–Oklahoma border. Over 40,000 square miles of water and home to more than 70 species of fish. If a 5 year old using a homemade fishing pole was able to catch buckets of trout with a stick, imagine the success now using a brand new spinning rod and reel perfectly strung with 4-pound test! How many trout do you think could be caught in a day? Hundreds? Hardly!

One could journey to Texoma day after day, fishing all 580 miles of shoreline or 89,000 acres of water, and never catch a single trout. Though fish are plentiful in Lake Texoma, there are no trout. Many fish could be caught, but if one is trying to catch trout, you'll have no luck trout fishing in Lake Texoma!

Recruiting is similar to fishing—it's essential to make sure you are recruiting the right candidates from the right source. Just because there is a body of water does not necessarily mean there any fish (or the ones you are looking for). As a good fishing guide helps fishermen improve the chance of a successful catch, a detailed hiring profile helps the S.M.A.R.T. manager focus the recruiting efforts on sources most likely to contain people meeting a specific hiring profile.

Effective Recruiting Sources

Years ago recruiting was as easy as "throwing out a net" and bringing in a large pool of applicants to interview. Simply place an ad in the local newspaper and plenty of resumes or applicants came pouring in. Today's hiring market is much different. Applicants are more savvy, and reaching them takes a more diverse approach.

As an employer it is important to identify all potential sources to generate the right applicant flow. These recruiting sources are listed in order of priority as well as cost effectiveness—the sources producing the best hires are often the most cost efficient.

- Internal
- Referrals
- Networking
- Job Boards
- Ads (Print and Internet)
- Recruiting Firms

Internal

Sometimes the obvious answer is the hardest to see. While tenacity helps improve the chance of success, focusing on the right "lake" can be much more effective. A fisherman can visit Lake Texoma over and over again, believing this large lake will eventually land a trout.

However, much closer to home is a small community lake stocked with trout every year for local residents to enjoy catching. S.M.A.R.T. managers look close to home for candidates first (like fishing in the right lake for the right type of fish). When searching for applicants who most closely fit the hiring profile, the most challenging aspect S.M.A.R.T. managers may experience is finding those candidates who are a fit with the culture and values of the company—the ones who will truly "fit in".

Anytime a new candidate is hired from "the outside" (even when they fit the hiring profile) there is a honeymoon period as they assimilate to the new company and culture. This process takes time, and to a degree, slows down the new hire's development in other areas.

TROUT FISHING ON LAKE TEXOMA

The advantage of promoting internally (once properly trained) is that they already function within the culture. The trade-off? Often, internally promoted people have less experience and may require more training on leadership and "soft skills". Many times, however, the learning curve is shortened due to the fact that there is such a strong cultural fit.

Internally promoted employees tend to be more loyal and less likely to leave quickly. The S.M.A.R.T. manager will always look internally *first* when filling a position. To maximize success (and shorten the learning curve), the S.M.A.R.T. manager will have a structured cross-training program to provide a developmental path for all employees.

Companies, such as Chipotle and S.M.A.R.T. Restaurant Group, strive for 80–100% of recruits to be internal promotes. While difficult to achieve during periods of high growth, being committed to training employees to be trainers, trainers to be supervisors and so on, allows S.M.A.R.T. managers to have qualified people ready to move up the ladder.

In doing so, the S.M.A.R.T. manager makes sure his pond is always stocked with the right kind of fish. Imagine how easy it is to catch a fish from a pond in one's own backyard. Internal promotions can be that "fully stocked pond". Be S.M.A.R.T.—create your own "pond" full of "trout" ready to be promoted within the restaurant!

Referrals

As mentioned earlier, cultural fit takes time. Any recruiting source aiding with cultural fit is the most effective. After internal promotions, the next most effective way to find those sharing similar values is through employee referrals. Want to find someone who shares the same values? Look within! Too often, managers neither develop promotable employees from within, nor seek referrals from current employees.

The S.M.A.R.T. manager will actively seek referrals from current staff—specifically the top performing staff members. Often, employees associate with people who would be a great fit for the restaurant, but are unaware the restaurant is looking for help (or to upgrade some of the current staff).

S.M.A.R.T. managers offer compensation, such as a referral bonus, for employees who refer candidates. By doing so, the S.M.A.R.T. manager creates a continuous recruiting source of like-minded candidates. When setting up such a program, include the following parameters:

- The candidate must be hired to earn a bonus.
- Provide multiple bonus payments based on the new hire's tenure. For example, one-third of payment at hire, one-third after training, and the final one-third after 90 days; don't drag it out too long.
- Provide a larger referral bonus for hard-to-fill positions, if needed.

The S.M.A.R.T. manager has a budget for recruiting efforts, and the referral bonus must work within the overall recruiting budget. But how much is enough?

Cost Per Hire

Cost per hire (CPH) is simply the total recruiting budget divided by the number of hires. For example, if a restaurant spends $6,000 over the course of a year and hired three managers, the CPH is $2,000. So far, internal promotions and referrals have been cited as effective recruiting costs. Internal promotions cost virtually nothing to recruit. In addition, referrals are very cost-effective recruiting sources.

Once the CPH is known, set the referral bonus amount to be mutually beneficial for all (MBA)—a win for the referring employee and a win for the restaurant. For example, a referral bonus of $1,000 is a great deal for the referring employee as well as the restaurant.

For hourly referrals, the bonus may be $25–$100, depending on the position (part- or full-time, closer, etc.). Referral bonuses, even for hourly staff, are far less expensive than running short-handed, which creates employee burn-out, paying overtime or providing less-than-stellar service. Pay now or pay much more later—you choose.

Referrals are a powerful recruiting source that a S.M.A.R.T. manager should not overlook.

Networking

Networking is another recruiting source that produces a higher percentage of applicants meeting the hiring profiles. S.M.A.R.T. managers use networking as it is generally low cost or no-cost—simply a manager's time. The S.M.A.R.T. manager identifies those networks surrounding the restaurant, which consists of members who fit the hiring profile. As with fishing, nothing is caught if there are no hooks in the water. Networking is one more "hook" (actually numerous hooks if done properly) in the water. S.M.A.R.T. managers wear their logo/brand when out in the market, at neighborhood events or chamber of commerce functions. Being involved in the local community is not only an effective marketing strategy, it is an effective *recruiting* strategy. One never knows when they will run into the next great candidate (or someone who knows a great candidate), so be in the marketplace, be involved and be on the lookout for talent! Have those business cards ready to provide to a potential star!

As with seeking referrals from *our* best employees, S.M.A.R.T. managers seek referrals from *any* employee who exhibits the right qualities and traits. How does it work? Simple—provide them a business card and say something along the lines of, "Hi, my name is [INSERT YOUR NAME] and I manage the [INSERT RESTAURANT NAME] restaurant down the street. I couldn't help but notice what an outstanding job you are doing today. Here is my card. If you have any friends who can work like you and are looking for a job please pass my card on them." The hook is in the water….

Schools

High schools, community colleges and universities can provide multiple networks of recruiting sources for entry-level or part-time positions.

The explosion of the Internet has opened many doors for recruiting. All schools have websites with links to organizers of the clubs and departments within the schools. Many high schools have a culinary or restaurant management/hospitality program, an obvious networking opportunity. Perhaps high school theater students, cheerleaders, athletes or other extra-curricular student groups have applicants who fit the hiring profile. Contact the department heads, volunteer to do a class on how to interview or see if they host a job fair or career day. Provide a reason for the school to get you face time with the students. A good source to produce a more experienced candidate is the hotel and restaurant management department at many community colleges or universities.

Social Media

The popularity of social media has significantly increased networking reach. With fishing you have to physically be at the lake to catch something. The web and social media are similar to "virtual fishing", allowing one to "catch" qualified applicants without physically having to be in the various locations.

Popular social media sites, such as Facebook, Twitter and LinkedIn, give exposure to hundreds or thousands of qualified applicants in the area around the restaurant. Best of all, recruiting via social media can attract applicants who may not currently be looking for a job, but they come across your company and "get hooked".

So how can the power of these sites be realized? Simply ask each of the employees to post on their Facebook page that the restaurant is looking to hire an experienced server (or whatever position needed). Cost? Zero (perhaps a referral bonus). Cost-effective exposure? If only half the employees (say 25 for this example) make the post, and each employee has 75 "friends" (they usually are far more connected), the message reaches 1,875 people. What if 10% of those "friends" passed the message on to their "friends"?

As the message goes viral the number of people made aware of the opportunity can escalate to the tens of thousands.

Taking it one step further, imagine some employees (with guidance and approval of the management) producing a short 2- to 3-minute video highlighting the cool work environment. Now the Tweet or Facebook post contains a link to a video showing what it's like to work in the restaurant. Keep it fun and upbeat, and the message helps sell the company to potential applicants for little or no cost. S.M.A.R.T. mangers think beyond typical uses for social media to send the message out in a cool, "magnetic" way to attract the right type of applicant!

While technology is everywhere, do not lose sight of plain, old-fashioned "networking". The S.M.A.R.T. manager always carries a stack of business cards—you never know when you might come across a person who is really impressive.

The S.M.A.R.T. manager utilizes multiple networking sources for their recruiting needs, and is constantly looking to increase the size of the network. Networking can produce a steady stream of candidates in a highly cost-effective manner.

Job Boards

Job boards can be an effective recruiting source, but are further down the list as they can be less cost-effective than the previously discussed sources. Generally, job board posts last 60 to 90 days and are a good source of applicants for hourly as well as management positions.

Job board companies, such as www.Snagajob.com, advertise where the job applicants are—schools, online and at events frequented by the 18- to 25-year-old crowd such as concerts.

Snagajob is the largest part-time and hourly job recruitment website, with over a quarter million listings. They are a premier go-to source for part-time and hourly job seekers, including hourly supervisors or shift managers. Applicants like sites such as this one as they can search by zip code or be notified when a new job posts in their area or desired field of work. As with any job board, Snagajob can prove to be most cost-effective when used by an operator with multiple locations and can be linked to attitude surveys or a company website, which allows the applicant to go through the proper application process and an immediate email is sent to the restaurant or manager.

For management-level or above-store level recruiting, the two most effective job boards are Monster and CareerBuilder. In addition to producing consistent applicant flow, they both include tools to help the recruiting manager manage and filter resumes.

Ads (Print and Internet)

Ads can still prove effective at recruiting for all levels. Be cautious, however, as print ads can be the least cost-effective form of recruiting. With newspaper readership at historically low levels (and dropping), try to avoid the large, citywide newspapers.

Print ads in smaller city or local papers can still produce applicants. High school and college papers are also cost-effective and targeted, if looking for candidates to fill specific positions such as part-time or seasonal work. S.M.A.R.T. managers highlight an existing employee in a school or local paper ad celebrating their success. Potential applicants seeing a non-traditional "recruiting" ad such as this one will respond more favorably, as the message in the ad is one of celebrating employees versus "now hiring".

S.M.A.R.T. managers understand how the effectiveness of ads is tied to the level of involvement the restaurant has in the local community, as well as how well known and established it is. Putting an ad in the paper is one thing but if nobody knows who you are or where you are located, why would they apply (other than if "they need a job"). S.M.A.R.T. managers want to hire cultural fits—people who love the food and want to wear the uniform proudly. If not properly placed or combined with marketing efforts, newspaper ads are often equivalent to "trout fishing in Lake Texoma".

The Internet is a more cost-effective means to getting the ad seen by a large numbers of people. Craigslist and other similar sites are a very cost-effective, fast and easy way to place an employment ad. In most markets for $25–$35, an ad can be posted in minutes. Job seekers at all levels refer to Craigslist for local employment opportunities. The downside? Internet ads are like fishing with a large net—the right fish may be caught but you will have to "fish through" a large number of the wrong fish. But, as the saying goes, "fish where the fish are biting".

Recruiting Firms

Third party recruiting firms can also be a valuable recruiting source and are most helpful for sourcing candidates such as Chef/Sous Chef, General Manager, Multi-Unit and above.

TROUT FISHING ON LAKE TEXOMA

In choosing a recruiting firm, S.M.A.R.T. managers understand how the firm recruits and whether or not their process will be complementary to the restaurant's approach.

For example, some recruiting firms simply source applicants through the use of ads, job boards and databases. They generally prescreen candidates to the employer's specifications. This type of process can be helpful to an employer who possibly does not have the time to interview multiple candidates. Keep in mind, however, the recruiting firm is essentially fishing from the same pond the manager could be fishing from. So it may not be economical, for example, to use a job board and this type of recruiting firm at the same time, as the sourcing pools will likely be redundant.

S.M.A.R.T. managers (when needed) utilize a recruiting firm that specializes in direct recruiting efforts as they are fishing from a completely different pond. These firms have access to candidates who generally do not respond to job boards and employment ads. A direct recruiting firm is an excellent source when recruiting for General Manager or above store-level positions.

The S.M.A.R.T. manager maintains several different recruiting sources. Of course, which sources they use at any given time depends upon what position(s) they are currently recruiting. But what do the ads look like?

Effective Ads

Regardless of where an employment ad is placed it must be effective, generating the right type of applicant flow. While there is no "silver bullet ad" guaranteed to produce traffic, an effective employment ad accomplishes two things:
1. Produces plenty of applicant flow, and
2. Produces relevant applicants

The employment ad should not ramble. A good ad articulates key aspects of the company culture; it does not contain a bunch of buzzwords meaningless to those outside the company. The ad should be as brief as possible and answer two primary questions for the potential applicant:

1. What does the position offer (culture, development, advancement, quality of life, recognition, benefits)?
2. What does the position require (experience level, skills, certifications, etc.)?

These two questions weigh most on a potential applicant's mind. Since print ads are expensive, don't forget about creating "video ads" placed on strategic websites or links. S.M.A.R.T. managers keep print ads short and focused on the two key questions potential applicants have. The ads will have a link or QR code taking the applicant into more of a visual overview of the restaurant to help better paint the picture of a "day in the life" working at the restaurant and showcases the culture. Why? To help better find the right like-minded individuals and stand out from all the advertising clutter!

Utilizing these recruiting sources begins the applicant flow. Ready to hire? Almost! Before one can actually select new employees, S.M.A.R.T. managers have a defined application process.

CHAPTER 4

A FEW HOOPS
NEVER HURT ANYONE

S.M.A.R.T. managers hate red tape. Because restaurant managers have a service mentality, they generally take steps to make the application process as easy as possible for potential candidates. To the S.M.A.R.T. manager, however, a few hoops never hurt anyone. The application process is the *beginning* of the screening process. When possible, the S.M.A.R.T. manager will create an application process to eliminate the unqualified candidates early, thereby leaving the most qualified candidates to compete for the position.

Application Types

Paper Applications

It's hard to believe paper applications are still around but this tried-and-true method still serves a purpose for many restaurants. The S.M.A.R.T. manager who uses the paper application will require the application to be completed in pen, legibly and completely. These clear directions should be given to the applicant when the application is given out. The applicant's ability to follow these three simple directions is step one in the screening process.

Online Applications

The use of technology in the application process can be a significant time saver for the S.M.A.R.T. manager, as well as another filter for the screening process. S.M.A.R.T. managers appreciate the online application process because it takes a little more effort for an applicant to complete. Less-motivated individuals will not take the time necessary to complete the application (helping minimize the risk of hiring someone who does not fit the culture).

Additionally, managing and filing applications becomes much easier when the applications are in electronic form. The use of attitude surveys in the application process is made easy when utilizing an online application. The next chapter covers how the S.M.A.R.T. manager best uses an attitude survey as a tool to help in the candidate screening process.

The Hiring Process

The complete hiring process is an important aspect of successfully selecting superior employees who fit the hiring profile. The S.M.A.R.T. manager has a thorough hiring process but moves quickly. The S.M.A.R.T. manager also understands that a *quick* hiring process does not mean an *easy* hiring process. After all, becoming a member of a superior team should be a bit difficult. Every restaurant position (including entry-level) should follow a S.M.A.R.T. hiring process consisting of at least the following 6 steps:

1. Complete the application
2. Attitude survey
3. First interview
4. Reference check
5. Second interview
6. Decision

Many managers follow a simpler, 3-step process: complete the application, interview and make a decision. In fact, the manager in the opening story of this book likely followed this 3-step hiring process. But the S.M.A.R.T. manager recognizes that a more thorough hiring process is a critical step toward writing a happy ending.

Though it is a 6-step hiring process, it can and should move quickly. The S.M.A.R.T. manager sets a maximum time line from receipt of application to final decision. For hourly positions within the restaurant, the process should not exceed 5 days. Each step of the hiring process should be built into the weekly managers' schedule. For example,

- Monday—review applications and set up interviews
- Tuesday—first interviews are complete
- Wednesday—second interviews completed
- Thursday—conduct reference checks
- Friday—make decisions and offers

By having a consistent process built into the weekly schedule, it assures the process keeps moving at an acceptable pace. Skeptical managers may think at this point, "Well I don't have time for that every week". They are right—they are too busy putting out fires and dealing with day-to-day issues of running the business operation!

The S.M.A.R.T. manager creates time in the weekly schedule for thoroughly screening applicants. The S.M.A.R.T. manager knows he will make no decision that is more important than whether or not to hire *each* one of the individuals who have applied. The hiring process must be structured in a way that gives the S.M.A.R.T. manager the maximum amount of information necessary to make those important decisions. With the hiring process well thought through and planned, the S.M.A.R.T. manager is ready to interview.

The final 4 steps of the process—the first and second interview, reference checks and the decision are covered later in this chapter.

It's Showtime

A lot of preparation has gone into getting to the interview portion of the process. Much thought and planning went into the number of people to hire, the specific positions to be filled and the exact attributes each person must have. Next, various targeted recruiting sources have produced a number of applicants. The stack of applications and/or attitude surveys have been combed over and interviews have been scheduled—it's showtime!

It's time to focus on gathering as much information about each applicant as possible. In planning and executing a good interview, the S.M.A.R.T. manager knows the interview is a *two-way,* fact-finding mission. The restaurant is gathering information to assess each candidate, while each candidate is gathering information to assess the restaurant. The candidate will make judgments about a potential employer based on the interview process. Was the process organized, professional, friendly and informative? Both the candidate and employer have a vested interested in making a good first impression.

Each interview should be well planned. As the hiring process indicates, each candidate is to be interviewed two times, ideally by two different people. Why? It is important to get a "second-opinion"— more than just one person's assessment of a candidate. Different interview styles and different lines of questioning will yield different information about each candidate. The S.M.A.R.T. manager's objective is to gather the maximum amount of information to make the most informed decision.

In a two-interview process, the ultimate decision maker should perform the second interview. Each step of the hiring process is intended to filter out candidates, leaving only the most qualified candidates for a second interview. When planning and scheduling interviews it is important to consider who is performing each interview.

The S.M.A.R.T. manager schedules interviews not only when convenient for the manager but also at a time relevant to the position being filled. Need a prep cook? Schedule the interview at 8:00 a.m. in the morning. Can the applicant be punctual for an early morning interview, be alert and function well in the mornings? The timing of interviews is an important part of gathering relevant information and should not be the same for all positions.

When staging an interview it is important not only to consider at what time the interview will be conducted, but also the exact location of where the interview will take place. The time of the interview often dictates where to conduct the interview in the restaurant. Whenever possible the

S.M.A.R.T. manager will pick an area a reasonable distance from the spot where the interviewer and candidate will first meet—for example, interview at a table very far from the front door. In fact the greater the distance of travel, the better. We discuss the reason for this later in this chapter.

The S.M.A.R.T. manager is fully prepared for the arrival of each candidate.

- Existing employees are made aware an interview is being conducted and the name of the applicant.
- The manager is prepared with the application, resume (if applicable), hiring profile, attitude survey and a pen and paper for notes (don't write on the application).
- "Punch out" with the staff—remind them not to interrupt the interview if at all possible so full attention can be devoted to the applicant.

The S.M.A.R.T. manager has carefully staged and prepared for the interview—it's showtime!

Interview Steps

The goal of the interview is to gather as much information as possible about each candidate. The S.M.A.R.T. interview consists of 8 stages:

1. Introduction
2. Travel path
3. Disarm
4. Personal
5. Background
6. Technical
7. Cultural
8. Ending

Introduction

The introduction is time for first impressions. As the S.M.A.R.T. manager approaches the candidate, information is already being gathered. The S.M.A.R.T. manager pays attention to the body language and image/appearance of the candidate. Does the candidate smile and make eye contact during introductions? Does the candidate have a firm, confident handshake? Likewise, is the handshake and tone of voice assertive or meek? Does the applicant come across as gregarious and welcoming, or more businesslike? The S.M.A.R.T. manager will make note of these first impressions...guests certainly do!

Travel Path

In the staging process, the S.M.A.R.T. manager picked a location to conduct the interview as far away from the spot of introduction as possible. Why? To help gauge if the applicant shares the S.M.A.R.T. manager's pace and sense of urgency as the manager quickly walks across the restaurant to the interview spot. Before sitting down to begin talking, S.M.A.R.T. managers have already gathered more information about the candidate.

Disarm

Every candidate comes to the interview with their guard up expecting to be questioned, poked and prodded. During this step of the interview process the S.M.A.R.T. manager wants to disarm the candidate by putting them at ease. Start by offering a soft drink and making sure the applicant is comfortable.

Next, begin by talking about something completely non-business related—weather, sports or a recent current event. Make small talk. The S.M.A.R.T. manager's objective is to get the applicant to feel they are having a conversation versus an interview. The more comfortable the applicant becomes, the more information he or she is likely to share.

A FEW HOOPS NEVER HURT ANYONE

Personal

As a natural transition from disarming the candidate, the next step is to get to know the candidate personally. What do they like to do when not at work? What are their hobbies? The S.M.A.R.T. interviewer will even share some of his or her own personal interests when appropriate in the conversation. This step further reinforces for the applicant the feeling of a conversation versus an interview. It's amazing what can be learned about someone by simply asking, "Tell me about yourself." The S.M.A.R.T. interviewer can learn many things about what motivates this person, their goals or future plans and much more. The S.M.A.R.T. interviewer is aware of certain personal questions that are irrelevant to the hiring decision, and inappropriate in the eyes of the law. These include questions about national origin, citizenship, age, marital status, disabilities, arrest and conviction record, military discharge status, race, gender or pregnancy status.

Background

Next, the S.M.A.R.T. interviewer focuses on the applicant's work background. The goal here is to thoroughly understand the previous positions the candidate has held. The S.M.A.R.T. interviewer asks questions targeted around the responsibilities and job duties the candidate has previously performed, as well as exact dates of employment, salary history and reasons for leaving past jobs. The S.M.A.R.T. interviewer ensures there is no ambiguity in the answers to any of these questions. S.M.A.R.T. managers do not accept broad, general answers. For example, if a candidate states they had to leave a job for "personal reasons", the S.M.A.R.T. interviewer will ask what those reasons were. It is important during this stage of the interview to develop a clear understanding of the candidate's experience and work history.

Technical

Based on the information gathered about the applicant's work background, the S.M.A.R.T. interviewer now asks questions to learn how skilled or technically sound the candidate may be. For example, if interviewing a candidate with experience as a kitchen expediter, ask what the most popular appetizer, entrée and dessert was in the restaurant. Then ask the applicant to walk through step-by-step how they plated each of these dishes.

If interviewing a Kitchen Manager who was responsible for food cost, ask questions such as "What food cost did you achieve and how did you do it?" During this stage of the interview the S.M.A.R.T. interviewer is determining whether the work experience and background of the candidate translates to the technical skills necessary to fill the open position.

Cultural

This stage of the interview is crucial and proves to be the most difficult for many interviewers. Much of the hiring profile for each position consists of qualities and traits. These are much harder to determine than whether or not a cook knows the difference between a rare and medium rare steak. The S.M.A.R.T. interviewer is trying to understand exactly how the candidate might work and interact with peers, subordinates, superiors and guests.

How will this candidate behave under different circumstances and conditions? The best predictor of how someone may behave in the future is how they have behaved in the past. Therefore, the S.M.A.R.T. interviewer will ask questions to determine a candidate's past behaviors. These questions will follow two rules of thumb:

- The questions will not be hypothetical
- The questions will not be close-ended (yes/no or one-word answers)

First, if a manager asks a hypothetical question they will get a hypothetical answer. Questions, such as "How would you deal with an upset guest?", are avoided as the applicant can respond with a stock answer. Savvy applicants know how to answer standard questions. Managers who need to fill staffing shortages are eager to hear what they want to hear. When they do, they "hire away", yet weeks or months later scratch their head wondering why the applicant did not work out. The S.M.A.R.T. interviewer deals only in the reality of real experiences. Instead, questions are framed to find out past behavior. Examples include:

- "The last time an employee came in late (or out of uniform), what did you do?"
- "Tell me about a time that you felt pressure at work to take a shortcut of some sort."
- "Tell me about a time when you disagreed with a supervisor."
- "Tell me about the most difficult guest you have ever had to deal with."

The S.M.A.R.T. interviewer asks a series of questions to determine how the candidate has behaved in different circumstances, but never leads them to an answer with a closed-ended question such as "Have you ever argued with a guest?"

The S.M.A.R.T. interviewer is disciplined, asking only questions that are specific in nature and only accepting specific answers. The S.M.A.R.T. interviewer may ask, "Tell me about the most difficult guest you have ever had to deal with." If the candidate's response is, "The guest is always right. I always just apologize and take care of the situation," the response does not answer the question at all.

The interviewer asked to hear about a specific situation. The S.M.A.R.T. interviewer *might* ask the question one more time, but generally a vaguely answered question is an unanswered question. The S.M.A.R.T. interviewer is not trying to figure out what the candidate *knows,* but rather how the candidate *behaves.* The S.M.A.R.T. interviewer will refer to the Hiring Profile to ensure a full assessment has been made (*see* Hiring Profile form on page 40).

By this stage of the interview, the S.M.A.R.T. interviewer should be ready to end the interview by going in one of two directions.

Ending

By using the hiring profile as a guide, the S.M.A.R.T. interviewer is ready to make one of two decisions.

1. Progress this candidate to a second interview (or make an offer if it is the second interview), or
2. end the process right here.

Not Extending an Offer

If the candidate does not meet the hiring profile, close the interview to allow the candidate to leave with dignity. Let them down easy but ensure they know they are not being offered a position at this time. For example, "Thank you for visiting with me today. We have several more interviews. I will be sharing my notes with the General Manager and the most qualified candidates will be called back. If you do not hear from us by Friday, we did not have a position meeting your needs at this time."

Extending an Offer

If the applicant does meet the hiring profile then a second interview should be set (or make an offer at the second interview if references have already been checked).

When ending a first interview, "sell" the candidate on the position. That is, get the candidate excited about working for the restaurant. The S.M.A.R.T. interviewer will take time to learn what is important to the candidate. The applicant wants to advance to a Kitchen Manager position? The S.M.A.R.T. interviewer might end the first interview by saying, "I really appreciate you taking the time to visit with me today. I feel strongly that your background is what we are looking for in a cook who could advance to a kitchen trainer and then KM position. I would like to schedule you for a second interview with my General Manager."

When closing the interview and selling the candidate, remember—your restaurant is likely not the only one the candidate is interviewing with for a position.

Immediately following the interview the S.M.A.R.T. interviewer will complete an assessment of the candidate. Assess the strengths and potential weaknesses of the candidate relative to the hiring profile. It is important to have good interview notes to share with the person who will be conducting the second interview. For example, see the notes on the Interview Assessment (on page 40).

At this point in the process, the attitude survey is best utilized to help validate what the interviewer determined were the candidate's strengths and weaknesses. If there are conflicting opinions between the attitude survey and the interviewer, the second interviewer has specific areas to focus on during the interview.

The second interview should flow in similar fashion to the first interview. This time, the manager has the advantage of the notes from the first interview and the attitude survey if one is used. S.M.A.R.T. interviewers wisely use this information to guide the interview and focus on areas that remain in question or are unknown. By the end of this second interview the S.M.A.R.T. manager should be able to clearly access whether or not the candidate meets the hiring profile.

HIRING PROFILE FOR: COOK

This opening is:

__ seasonal

_x_ permanent

__ part time

_x_ full time

Experience required:
2 years

Pay range:
$10.00–$12.00/hour

Service-oriented

Desire to improve/advance

Results-oriented

Decisive

Drive/energy

Urgency

Attention to detail

Ability to multi-task

INTERVIEW ASSESSMENT

	Strength	**Average**	**Weakness**
Service-oriented		X	
Desire to improve/advance	X		
Results-oriented		X	
Decisive		X	
Drive/energy		X	
Urgency			X
Attention to detail		X	
Ability to multi-task	X		

NOTES:

1. Bob is an average candidate overall with 2.5 years cook experience

2. He wants to find a job where he can advance into management

3. He frequently operates the grill in his current position while running the fry station, showing an ability to multi-task

4. He was lethargic through interview; seems lacking in urgency—perhaps this is why he has not advanced with his current employer.

CHAPTER 5
DON'T LET THEM DIE ON THE VINE

The last step of the hiring process is to verify the candidate's references. Many times reference checks can be completed between the first and second interview to keep the process moving quickly. When checking references it is best to speak with a direct supervisor from a previous job. Avoid speaking with someone from Human Resources, as they will just provide you with salary and date information. Have the candidate provide you with a direct phone number for their previous supervisor.

In addition, it is a good idea to instruct the candidate to let their references know that you will be calling them. This step will frequently speed up the process on your end by reducing the number of calls necessary to make contact. The S.M.A.R.T. manager is prepared for the reference check with a list of specific questions to ask. Just as when interviewing the candidate, ask specific questions when doing a reference check to focus in on the behavior of the candidate.

What were Bob's strengths? What did Bob need improvement on? Was Bob punctual? Would you rehire Bob? Why did Bob leave your employ? Listen closely to the responses. Answers that are vague are a red flag. The S.M.A.R.T. manager takes good notes as to provide one last important piece of information to aid in the hiring decision.

If possible, mystery-shop the candidate where they are currently employed. What they do is far more important than what they say. Visit their current place of employment as a guest to see what the restaurant or store looks like and how the shift is operating, especially in the area of service. Employees out of uniform, dirty tables or no management presence on the floor? That's what you will be hiring!

Alternatively, provide a meal pass or reimbursement and have the candidate mystery-shop your restaurant and discuss with you their observations. This process will help you better understand what they observe, if they provide solutions or suggestions and how they react to both positive and negative items they witnessed.

Once that step is accomplished, then the process should be complete at this point—no need to delay making a hiring decision.

The S.M.A.R.T. manager has all of the information necessary to make a good hiring decision and moves quickly to extend an offer to those candidates who meet the hiring profile. The truly exceptional candidates will get other offers, so the S.M.A.R.T. manager moves quickly to put an end to the candidate's search.

In addition to a well thought-out hiring process, the S.M.A.R.T. manager also has an effective on-boarding system. Even though a candidate accepts an offer, he or she may receive additional offers prior to starting with your company. If the candidate is currently employed and giving notice, the probability is high they will receive a counter-offer. An effective on-boarding process can help insure the candidate is not lost to a competing employer.

Changing jobs or starting a new job is a stressful and emotional time for most people. The S.M.A.R.T. manager takes steps toward making an emotional connection with the new employee even before day one. In doing this, the S.M.A.R.T. manager:

- invites the new hire to lunch one afternoon around the same time of the weekly staff meeting, taking the opportunity to introduce the new hire to the team;
- invites the new hire and their spouse to dinner one evening to get to know them;
- takes the opportunity to meet their parents (if the new hire is a minor), inviting the family in to eat at the restaurant so the parents can get comfortable with their child's place of employment (and get them on your side!);
- schedules the new hire's first day as quickly as possible.

DON'T LET THEM DIE ON THE VINE

The S.M.A.R.T. manager has just made the most important decision of the week for the restaurant by hiring this candidate—do not delay or let the applicant "die on the vine". So much work, planning and execution has led to this new employee starting with the team—ensure they do not go to work elsewhere in the interim. Keep in contact with the new hire to ensure he or she is clear on the starting day!

The S.M.A.R.T. manager invests plenty of time and effort into selecting the team. Although the daunting daily tasks of running a restaurant can be stressful at times, S.M.A.R.T. managers methodically move to greatness by selecting great people to be on their team. While every manager may have some people "misses" along the way, S.M.A.R.T. managers stay focused on the hiring profile. Regardless of the situation he or she is in, the S.M.A.R.T. manager stays focused and controls the outcome. The success through people ensures the S.M.A.R.T. manager is able to write a happy ending.

CONCLUSION
HAPPILY EVER AFTER

It's Monday morning, and I quickly do a mental review of what I need to accomplish as I pull into the restaurant parking lot for my opening shift. We had record sales last week, and I can't wait to share the results with the team. My opening cook is waiting for me at the front door, prompt as always.

As we walk through the kitchen I can't help but feel a sense of pride in a clean and well-organized restaurant. My Assistant Manager closed last night and, as usual, did a great job of leading the closing team toward another solid close. My opening cook jumps right on the morning fresh prep as I review the numbers from yesterday.

The phone rings and it is my Director of Operations calling to congratulate me on another record-breaking sales month for the restaurant. I follow up on my cook and all is going well. He informs me we need to increase our par level on crab-stuffed mushrooms due to the increased volume. I concur with his decision and told him to make the change.

As he is finishing up on the prep I review last week's applications. I am fully staffed right now, but according to my manpower plan I need to be on the lookout for a night-time server. I make some calls and set up first interviews for my Service Manager tomorrow afternoon.

Opening time is fast approaching so I huddle up with the FOH and BOH teams and set goals for the lunch shift. Everyone has clear direction and we are ready. Bring it on!

Lunch goes flawlessly. We are quite busy but my aces are in their places and the dining room is at capacity. After following up on the kitchen staff, I make my rounds through the FOH when a guest waves to get my attention. I hurry over to the table to see how I may be of assistance.

The guest wants to inform me the visit today was outstanding. They tried a new appetizer the server recommended and wanted to send their compliments to the kitchen. As I make my way to the hostess station to check on the wait, I thank a departing guest. They too make a point to praise the food and let me know how friendly and prompt their server was today.

As the shift winds down everyone hustles through the side work, and we begin the process of getting ready for the dinner rush. After an afternoon training session with the host staff and a quick meeting with the closing manager, the day is complete.

Leaving the parking lot I do a mental recap of the day—another solid team performance exceeding guests' expectations. Though it was a busy shift, full to capacity, the team was never stressed. We continue to set new sales records and are the most profitable restaurant in the company. What a far cry from those miserable days full of people headaches from long ago!

Recruit and select S.M.A.R.T. and write your happy ending!